Maureensbridal

www.Maureensbridalshop.com

Comfortably Ever After™

VERA WANG
BY SERTA®

Jahzara Saphir
BRIDAL MAGAZINE

Editor-in-chief **Princess Keith**

Design Editor	Donele Bailey
Fashion Director	Crystal Carmen
	Jeannie White
Advertising Directors	Princess Keith
Contributing Writer	Paris Giles
Contributing Photographer	Shawn Durley
	Frank Gay
	Anthony Williamson
	Sylvester Graham
	Joey Neas
	Bobby Weitzner
	Karissa Starcevich
	Bee Photography LLC
	BN Photography
Hair/ Makeup Beauty Team	Tenacious Glam

EDITORIAL OFFICE

5087 Edgewater Drive, Suite 608192
+1-813-331-5503 | Info@jahzarasaphirmagazine.com

Jahzara Saphir Bridal Magazine is published by Mocy Publishing Group.
Coming to a location near you! | +1-813-331-5503

www.jahzarasaphirmagazine.com

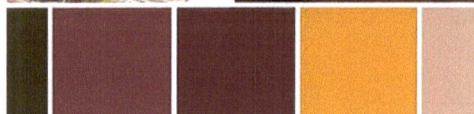

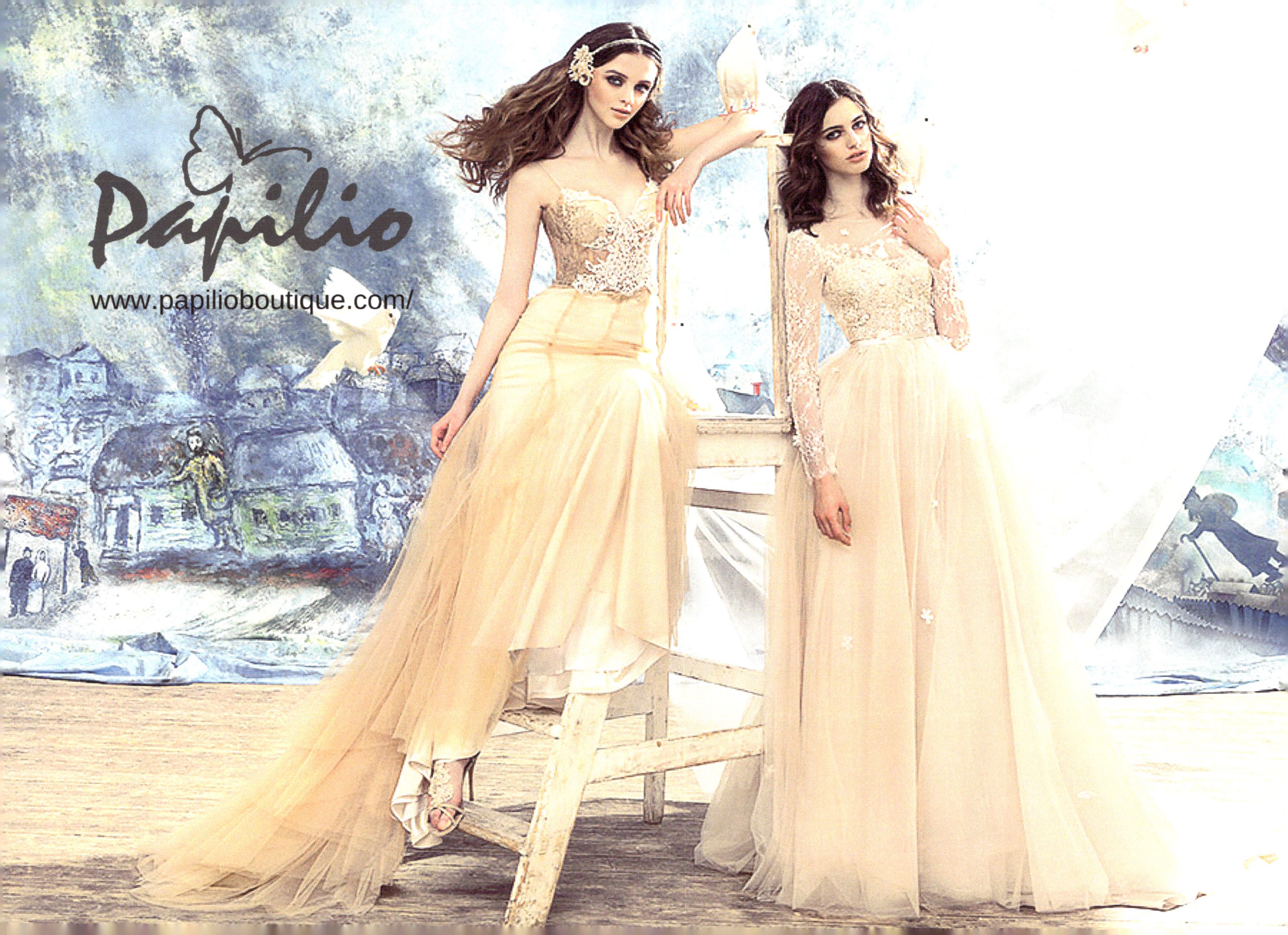
Papilio
www.papilioboutique.com/

WILL YOU KNOW THAT THE REASON I LAUGH WHEN
I'M WITH YOU ISN'T BECAUSE YOU'RE
SO FUNNY, ALTHOUGH YOU ARE? IT'S SIMPLY BECAUSE
SMILING CAN'T CONTAIN MY JOY.
WILL YOU KEEP LAUGHING WITH ME FOREVER?

WILL YOU?

TIFFANY & CO.

NEW YORK SINCE 1837

Baker Spotlight

Ana Paz's claim to fame is hard work, a Puerto Rican bloodline and a vanilla rum cake recipe circa 1916. Paz moved from San Juan with her grandmother's cake recipes and her mother's teachings in tow to Miami in 1978, and in the time since, she's founded Ana Paz Cakes– the go-to for premier wedding and event cakes in South Florida.

Past celebrity clients include Jennifer Lopez and Katie Holmes, and luxury area hotels frequently employ the bakery's services. Three months after she moved to Miami, Paz booked her first professional job with Marriott with only six photos in her portfolio. Even with big name employers, Ana Paz Cakes remains dedicated to those anxious, overwhelmed brides looking to dazzle guests with multi-tiered works of art that taste just as exquisite as they look.

That vanilla rum cake is Ana Paz Cakes' signature item. Paz and her team also create variations of the classic favorite made with hazelnut, guava or coconut. Whichever decadent dessert betrothed couples choose, the process is often tedious to ensure beautiful execution down to the minutest detail. Expect lots of communication.

Although Paz focuses her work in the Miami area, cakes can be shipped to any city to which United Airlines flies. Paz employees a service – the same one that ensures proper handling of organs, tropical fish and other packages that require special care – to be sure that the creations make it to their destinations deliciously intact.

Paz says it's her client service and her experience which sets her apart from other cake makers. She's been baking since eighth grade, and growing up, her mother baked wedding cakes on a small scale from their house in San Juan as well as dabbled in catering for cocktail parties and other events. This type of sugary saturation serves her clients well.

"It was naturally embedded in me," Paz said in a thick Puerto Rican accent. "I grew up with it."

But of course it's the taste that keeps Ana Paz's name and her sweet creations on people's lips and makes her one of the most sought-after wedding cake creators in the country. Whether covered in roses or festooned in pearls, each cake is made with fresh ingredients and a crafty hand and sure to pleasure the palate. Everything in Ana Paz Cakes' repertoire is also dairy-free and certified Kosher, and virtually unchanged from the original recipes.

Paz said, "Our cakes have been the same from my grandmother's kitchen in 1916 'til now."

- Paris Giles

WEDDING ♥ PLANNING GUIDE

12 Months or More
- ☐ Select a wedding date and time
- ☐ Decide the size and formality
- ☐ Announce engagement
- ☐ Agree on a preliminary budget
- ☐ Decide on expenses sharing
- ☐ Schedule appt. with Officiant
- ☐ Start your wedding guest list
- ☐ Select your reception location

9-12 Months Before
- ☐ Choose bridal attendants
- ☐ Choose your color schemes
- ☐ Engagement photos taken
- ☐ Select your videographer
- ☐ Select tuxedos
- ☐ Select your florist
- ☐ Select professional caterer
- ☐ Select any musicians
- ☐ Shop for wedding rings

6-9 Months Before
- ☐ Select your dress and headpiece
- ☐ Select bridesmaids' dresses
- ☐ Plan your reception
- ☐ Choose honeymoon destination
- ☐ Meet with your reception MC
- ☐ Select wedding cake

4-6 Months Before
- ☐ Check into marriage license
- ☐ Meet with the florist/decorator
- ☐ Reserve any rental equipment
- ☐ Order invitations and stationary
- ☐ Select transportation services
- ☐ Reserve hotel rooms for guests

2-4 Months Before
- ☐ Research ceremony readings
- ☐ Decide upon a gift registry
- ☐ Make music selections

2-4 Months Before
- ☐ Order favors and decorations
- ☐ Help mothers with clothing
- ☐ Review vendor contracts
- ☐ Announcement in newspaper
- ☐ Arrange the rehearsal dinner
- ☐ Purchase your accessories
- ☐ Select gifts for attendants
- ☐ Finalize order with florist
- ☐ Preliminary hair and makeup

1-2 Months Before
- ☐ Mail out invitations
- ☐ Finalize details
- ☐ Buy marriage license
- ☐ Final dress fittings
- ☐ Select ceremony accessories: candle, ring pillow, guest book
- ☐ Select personal accessories: purse, garter, toasting flutes
- ☐ Make salon appointments

2 Weeks Before
- ☐ Finalize with entertainers
- ☐ Provide music you want
- ☐ Pick up your wedding rings
- ☐ Check fit and engravings
- ☐ Finalize guest count
- ☐ Change of name and address

1 Week Before
- ☐ Men pick up formal wear
- ☐ Prepare seating arrangements
- ☐ Verify marriage license is in order
- ☐ Confirm honeymoon reservations
- ☐ Inform caterer total guest count
- ☐ Finalize transportation
- ☐ Vendor payments to best man
- ☐ Confirm hotel/travel plans
- ☐ Confirm details with florist

1 Day Before
- ☐ Pack the bridal emergency bag
- ☐ Wedding rehearsal and dinner
- ☐ Exchange gifts with your fiancé
- ☐ Get a good night's rest

Day of Wedding
- ☐ Have a nice relaxed breakfast
- ☐ Allow two hours or more to dress
- ☐ Allow time for makeup and hair
- ☐ Photographs before ceremony
- ☐ Get rings and marriage license
- ☐ Relax and enjoy your special day

12 Months (Groom)
- ☐ Select and purchase bride's rings
- ☐ Discuss of financial obligations with fiancé and parents
- ☐ Decide budget, date guest count
- ☐ Choose and secure reception

6-9 Months (Groom)
- ☐ Make reservations for honeymoon
- ☐ Arrangements for out-of-town guests
- ☐ Arrange bridal party transportation
- ☐ Choose best man and attendants

1-2 Months (Groom)
- ☐ Set a date to get marriage license
- ☐ Confirm rehearsal dinner reservations
- ☐ Help fiancé address invitations

1 Week (Groom)
- ☐ Confirm time/place of rehearsal and dinner with attendants
- ☐ Pick up engraved rings

Wedding Day (Groom)
- ☐ Pick up formal wear
- ☐ Relax and enjoy the day

Eddy K.

Eddy K.

WEDDING AND FITNESS APPS

Need a helpful app to plan your big day? Check out these apps to keep your stress level to a minimum.

1 FITOCRACY APP

Trim down for your walk down the aisle with Fitocracy. This app makes it easy to stay on top of being active; in fact, it turns physical fitness into a game. Track all your physical activities leading up to the wedding

2 FAST TALK BY LONELY PLANET

Wedding planning chaos left you without time to learn the language? Lonely Planet's phrasebook can help you get by. The free app comes with your choice of French, German, Italian, Latin American Spanish or European Spanish.

3 ZOLA REGISTRY

Zola is a (quite gorgeous) digital solution for curating a registry. The newly-released, photo-heavy mobile extension to the site has a Tinder-like feature — swipe right to add an item to your registry or left to pass it up. See something you covet on the go?

4 EVERNOTE

Stay organized across devices and individuals with Evernote. Share your notes with others — you and your spouse-to-be can update the same list. Better yet, assign to-do items to your significant other by color-coding.

5 PROJECT WEDDING

Create inspiration boards, share ideas with your friends and wedding vendors, get feedback from brides like you, and lots more!

6 WEDDING PARTY APP

Collect and organize all your pictures from your engagement party to the wedding day, without having to bug your loved ones individually. Keep your guests in the loop, from event schedule and directions to hotel and gift registries. Your guests will thank you. Plus no one will get lost on the way to the reception!

7 APPY COUPLE

Looking to consolidate all the info about your big day into one gorgeous package? Consider Appy Couple, an app and website. All of the info about your big day can live in the app, including event timelines, venue details, gift registries and even shareable blurbs about VIP guests. Guests can add photos via the app, complete with filter and effect options.

8 SPOTIFY

If a DJ isn't in the budget, consider using Spotify. With a little pre-planned playlist curation, simply connect your device of choice to speakers on the big day to get the tunes pumping.

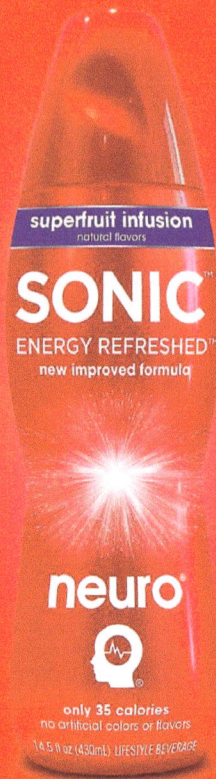

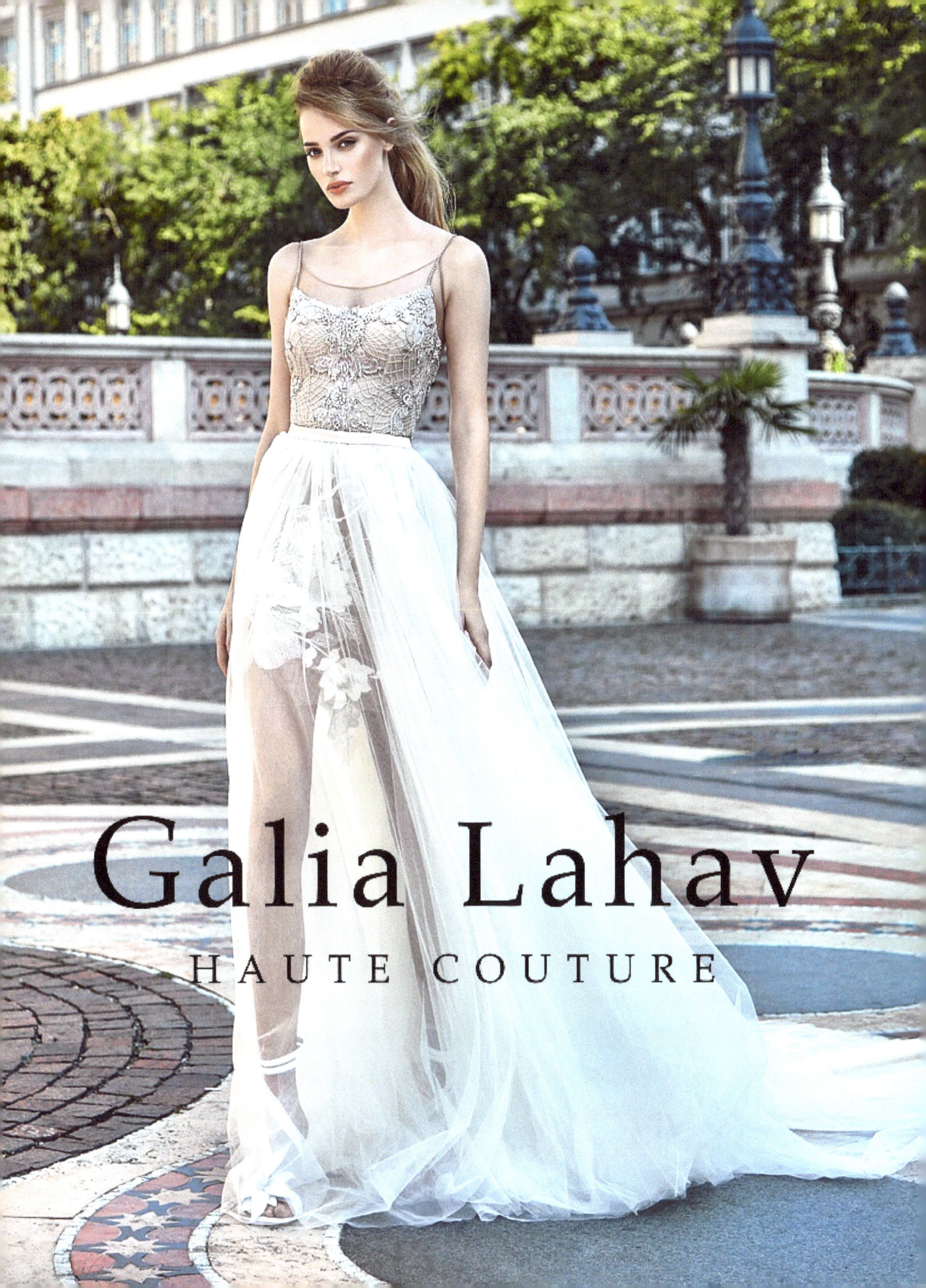

Galia Lahav

HAUTE COUTURE

HOW TO PLAN YOUR WEDDING IN 90 DAYS

LETS GET STARTED

3 MONTHS

Week 12:
Set a date and a few alternatives; establish a budget; get ideas and referrals for your site, food, honeymoon and soon from bridal magazines and friends; set up appointments with potential vendors and ceremony and reception sites for the next two weeks; shop for a gown.

Week 11:
Book your ceremony and reception venues and as many pros as you can; ask people to be in your bridal party; order invitations and rings; block out hotel rooms for out-of-town guests; book your honeymoon trip.

Week 10:
Hire any remaining vendors; buy dress and accessories; book appointments for a manicure and pedicure for the day before the wedding and a hair and makeup stylist for the big day; get blood tests, if required (talk to your officiant).

Week 9:
Send invitations; find bridesmaid dresses; send your fiancé to get tuxes for himself and his groomsmen.

2 MONTHS

Week 8: Register for gifts.

Week 7: Meet with the officiant to plan the ceremony.

Week 6: Meet with the caterer to taste foods and plan the menu; book limos.

Week 5: Create a music list for your bandleader; get your marriage license.

1 MONTH & COUNTING

Week 4: Have a dress fitting (you'll have to follow the store's schedule); make sure you have your accessories.

Week 3: Pick up rings.

Week 2: Contact guests who haven't responded to your invite; make reception seating arrangements.

Week 1: Pick up dress; confirm wedding services; give caterer final headcount; pack for the honeymoon

SIMPLE WORDING

The honor of your presence
is requested at the marriage of

Marion Bailey
and
Thomas Willamson

Saturday, the seventh of June
two thousand fourteen
at half past four in the
afternoon

The Prospect Pavilion
409 Ocean Parkway
Brooklyn, New York

Reception immediately to
follow
The Boathouse
163 Greenwood Avenue

TRADITIONAL WORDING

Mom Name
Dad & Step-Mom Name

request the pleasure of your
company
at the marriage of their daughter

Alexis Lee West
to
Taylor Eliot Keegan

son of
Other Mom Name and Step-Dad
Name
Other Dad Name

Saturday, the seventh of June
two thousand fourteen
at half past four in the afternoon

The Prospect Pavilion
409 Ocean Parkway
Brooklyn, New York

Dinner and dancing to follow

FUN WORDING

Alexis Lee West
and
Taylor Eliot Keegan

Are Gettin' Hitched!
Please join us
For a celebration of love,
friendship,
laughter, and family

Saturday, June 7, 2014
at 4:30 in the afternoon

The Prospect Pavilion
409 Ocean Parkway
Brooklyn, New York

Fabulous food, fun, and
festivities to follow

"Love is our true destiny. We do not find meaning of life by ourselves alone—we find it with another. - Thomas Merton"

Q&A: INVITE HELP

WHEN SHOULD WE SEND OUT OUR WEDDING INVITATIONS?

Traditionally, invitations go out six to eight weeks before the wedding -- that gives guests plenty of time to clear their schedules and make travel arrangements if they don't live in town. If it's a destination wedding, give guests more time and send them out three months ahead of time. Most couples also send out save-the-date cards. They go out at six to eight months.

IF OUR WEDDING RECEPTION IS FOR IMMEDIATE FAMILY ONLY, IS IT OKAY TO INVITE PEOPLE TO THE CEREMONY ONLY?

Everyone who attends the ceremony (or bridal shower, engagement party or wedding reception) should be invited to the wedding -- that means the ceremony and the reception.

VINTAGE *romance*

VICTORIA
&
NICHOLAS

As two families
Become one
that We ask
You choose a Seat
Not a Side

SOMETHING *woodsy*

YOU ARE
INVITED TO JOIN IN A
CELEBRATION
SARAH & CHASE
HANSEN ARNOLD

Sara
Danny

ALL ABOUT *dots*

BEST DAY
Ever

Luxe Print Shop

PAPERIE & MORE

Find us on
Facebook
@Luxeprintshop

LOVE

Wedding
Placemats & Coasters
Aisle Runners
Engagement
Save the Dates
Save the Date Magnets
Bridal Shower Invitations
Bridal Shower Accessories
Bachelor & Bachelorette
Party
Rehearsal Dinner
Wedding Invitations
Spanish Invitations
Same Sex
Luxe Material Invitations
Pockets
Seal 'n Sends™
Sep 'n Sends™
Reception Cards
RSVP Cards
Map & Accommodation
Cards

Programs
Guest Books & Pens
Unity Candles & Stands
Flower Girl Baskets
Ring Bearer Pillows
Place Cards
Personalized Napkins
Coasters
Menus
Favors
Table Numbers
Cake Toppers
Serving Sets
Toasting Flutes
Reception Decorations
Thank You Notes
Layers & Liners
Embellishments
Envelope Seals
Address Labels & Icing
Garters
Wedding Party Gifts
Keepsakes

Info@luxeprintshop.com
(321) 710-LUXE (5893)
www.luxeprintshop.com

Gino Cerruti
LONDON

About Us

GinoCerruti has the largest collection of evening dresses, bridal gowns, prom dresses and special occasion wear the United Kingdom. With rich and vibrant colours, the finest fabrics and the most elegant styles, there's no need to stress about finding the perfect dress for your formal occasion. We have a variety of hemlines, fabrics and colours to choose from so finding that dream evening dress has never been easier and more enjoyable. The London-based fashion house has developed a signature style of glamour and elegance, from fun and flirty designs in colours that stand out, to breathtaking styles that take more subtle colours, like black and silver, to the next level. GinoCerruti is quite simply turning every girl's dream of owning an amazing dress into a reality.

Our newest evening dress collection features a mix of styles, including lace and beading, strapless and A-line, as well as form-fitting mermaid gowns. Whether you're the hostess or a guest, don't limit yourself to the standard little black dress. Look elegant in a beaded cocktail dress with a tulle-layered wire hem skirt, or go classic in a lengthy, mermaid gown with a strapless sweetheart neckline. The options are endless. Prom 2016 is approaching fast and GinoCerruti is ready! With the largest prom collection in the UK, we have produced a new selection of prom dresses that goes beyond the normal ball gown and includes the latest trends perfect for any teenage-fashion lover. From strapless princess gowns that make you feel like a princess to slim fitting, figure-hugging dresses that include crystals and thigh-high slits, glamour is the first priority for GinoCerruti.

GinoCerruti's new special occasion wear collection features the latest styles of the season. With right mix of trendy and contemporary details, combined with classic styles, women all over the world have come to rely on GinoCerruti to dress them for their special occasion.

GinoCerruti wedding dresses already known for their beauty and elegance. Brides the world over are increasingly choosing to wear a GinoCerruti dress on one of the most important days of their lives. Like GinoCerruti pageant dresses and prom dresses, their wedding dresses and gowns mix contemporary style with tradition to produce gorgeous results. When it comes to choosing the right wedding dress, this is a unique occasion for you, the wearer. That means that getting the right mix of tradition and individuality is crucial. What's more, that extra dash of sexiness that GinoCerruti puts into their bridal gowns means no one is ever going to forget the way you look in your wedding dress.

All of our prom gowns, party dresses, cocktail dresses, evening gowns, bridal gowns, bridesmaid dresses, children's dresses and special occasion dresses are of the highest quality and come in an impressive range of sizes. We are constantly working hard to ensure that we produce and provide you with the finest possible garments.

GinoCerruti is one of the best-known evening and prom gowns, special occasion and bridal dresses company in the world. Make sure you don't miss this opportunity to discover our delightful dresses.

Gino Cerruti
LONDON

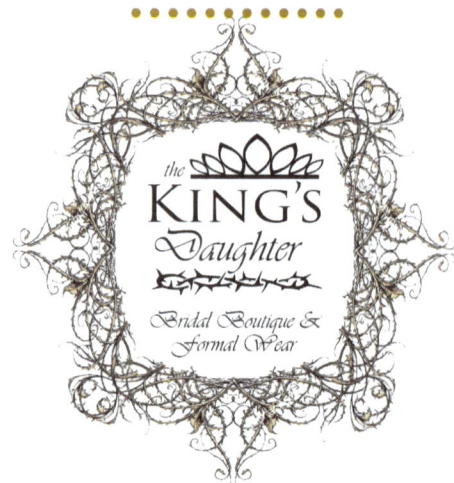

the KING'S Daughter
Bridal Boutique &
Formal Wear

Mon - Saturday 10am to 6pm
By appoinment only on Sundays

1900 Huntington Ln. - Rockledge

Phone: 321-536-7818

www.thekingsdaughterbridal.com

The Kings Daughter Bridal Boutique
bring uniqueness from London, England
to the USA. They carry an exclusive
Bridal & Formal line by Gino Cerruti.
"Gino Cerruti" amazing bridal line goes
by the name of Le Novia and is hand
crafted with 100% Authentic Silk Italian
Lace right from the heart of Italy. The
Kings Daughter Bridal is located in
Rockledge, Florida they offer this
exclusive designer "Gino Cerriti"
throughout the United States.

Bridesmaids

Mother of the bride

Shoes - Veils - Accessories

Garment preservation

Exclusive one of a kind Formal wear

Evening wear

Alterations

Flowers Girls

Custom Wedding Gowns & Designing

Prom & Formal

Contact us to find this exclusive designer

NEAR YOU

Image by: Fairytale Images

Custom Printed Eyewear

Pet Owner ◆ Notes

THESE ARE SOME WAYS YOU CAN INCLUDE YOUR PET:

- *Use your pet to propose.*
- *Include them in your engagement photos.*
- *Your wedding photos.*
- *Invite them to the ceremony. ...*
- *Give them a special job, like sign holder. ...*
- *Flower Girl escort or ring bearer.*

MAKE SURE EVERYONE ON YOUR GUEST LIST IS COMFORTABLE HAVING YOUR PET AROUND. YOU SHOULD CONSULT WITH YOUR SPOUSE-TO-BE, AND YOU MAY NEED TO ASK YOUR GUESTS DIRECTLY. IF YOUR FUTURE FATHER-IN-LAW HAS A CAT ALLERGY OR YOUR FLOWER GIRL IS TERRIFIED OF DOGS, LEAVE YOUR PET AT HOME.

PRACTICE, PRACTICE, PRACTICE. LIKE ANY TRICK OR NEW BEHAVIOR, YOUR WEDDING ROUTINE NEEDS TO BE REINFORCED FOR YOUR PET. TAKE IT SLOWLY AND KEEP IT POSITIVE. IF YOUR PET IS GOING TO BE WEARING A NEW ITEM, LIKE A BOW TIE COLLAR OR A RING PILLOW, PUT IT ON SEVERAL TIMES BEFORE THE ACTUAL EVENT. OFFER TREATS AND PRAISE, EVEN FOR JUST WEARING THE NEW ITEM. IF YOU CAN, PRACTICE A FEW TIMES IN THE ACTUAL LOCATION SO YOUR PET WILL BE FAMILIAR WITH IT. IF THE LOCATION ISN'T AVAILABLE, TRY PRACTICING IN LOTS OF DIFFERENT PLACE SO YOUR PET WILL FEEL CONFIDENT IN A STRANGE PLACE.

HOWEVER YOU DECIDE TO INCLUDE YOUR BFF IN YOUR BIG DAY, MAKE SURE TO DESIGNATE SOMEONE YOU TRUST TO BE IN CHARGE OF YOUR ANIMAL SO YOU CAN FOCUS ON THE FUN. YOU DON'T WANT THIS TO HAPPEN...

Signature

Pet Owners Note

GIVENCHY

Live Irrésistible

THE NEW EAU DE TOILETTE

SUBSCRIBE
& BE AMUSED.

Save over $45 off the newsstand price.

Give a subscription today and get the

current issue for free.

Fill out this card and send it with payment to Jahzara Saphir Magazine, PO Box 608192, Edgewater Dr., Orlando, FL 32860

SHIPPING INFORMATION

....
Name

....
Address

....
City   State   ZIP

....
Email   Mobile No.

Make checks payable to "Jahzara Saphir Magazine"
Credit card holders must be placed by Credit Car holders only.

BILLING INFORMATION

- Payment Scheme -

Credit Card   Check   Money Order

....
Credit Card No.

....
Expiry   CVC No.

....
Signature   Total in $

Please allow 12-14 days before the first issue to arrive. Do not send cash
Offer valid through June 30, 2020

JAHZARASAPHIRMAGAZINE.COM/SUBSCRIBE

Authentic
CAKE CITY

HAPPY HOUR

• *A wedding cocktail recipe you need to know* •

SPARKLE BOMB

Add this classic wedding signature drink to your arsenal and impress your friends!

- Pomegranate vodka
- Orange liqueur
- Pomegrante juice
- Lime twist
- With a sparkling sugar rim.

REAL
WEDDING

Tara + Spencer were married in downtown St. Louis in an ultra sleek and modern location. They paid close attention to details from the wedding cake to the decorations to the wedding party's ensembles. Everything truly sparkled...including their love for each other! Congratulations to Tara + Spencer.

The Dream Team:
Location: Palladium St. Louis www.palladium-stl.com
Caterer: Butler's Pantry www.butlerspantry.com
Cake: The Sweet Divine www.thesweetdivine.com
Floral: The Crimson Petal www.thecrimsonpetal.net
Linen: La Tavola www.LaTavolaLinen.com
Custom designed rentals: Millennium Productions
www.millenniumProductions.com
Lighting: from venue
Stationery: PaperCut Invites www.papercutinvites.com
Wedding gown designer: Olia Zavozina
www.oliazavozina.com via Simply Elegant Bridal
www.simplyelegantbridalstl.com
Groom's tuxedo: Jim's Formalwear via Simply Elegant
Veil/ headpiece Simply Elegant
www.simplyelegantbridalstl.com
Bride's shoes: Steve Madden
Entertainment: Brian at Millennium Productions
www.millenniumProductions.com
Cinematographer: Switzerfilm www.switzerworld.com
Photographer: Switzerfilm www.switzerworld.com
Snow Cone Bar: St. Louis Snow Cone
www.stlsnowcone.com

25 WEDDING VENUE QUESTIONS

- Do you have my date available?
- Will I have exclusive use of the venue?
- Are there any extra charges or restrictions for using the surrounding areas / lawns?
- If it is a multi-function site, how will privacy be maintained?
- What are your policies on deposits and cancellation fees?
- What is included in your wedding packages?
- Do you offer special deals for events on a weeknight or during 'off-peak' times of the year?
- What is the cut off time for music/entertainment and the event? What are the possibilities and costs for extending the deadline?
- Do you have a contingency for bad weather?
- If seated dinner, how much notice do you require for the menu selections?
- If buffet menu, what duration is it open for? What duration are canapés served for?
- What are the options in place for guests with special dietary requirements?
- Can I attend a food and wine tasting?
- Can I supply my own alcohol? If so, what is the corkage?
- How many service staff will be allocated for the wedding?
- Can I bring in external caterers for traditional dishes or wedding cake?
- What time would we have access to the venue for set-up? Would there be a charge for using the venue the day before?
- Is there sufficient access for deliveries? What time can suppliers gain access to the venue?
- Do you have a preferred supplier list? Can we bring in other external suppliers?
- Do you have any in-house AV equipment that's included in the package – speakers, mic, stage, basic lighting?
- Is there a dance floor? What size and how many can the dance floor hold?
- What furniture / linen inventory do you have? Colours, styles etc.
- Is valet parking included?
- Are there dressing facilities for the bridal party?
- Is there external cooling / heating (if relevant)?
- Can I see the venue set up for a wedding?

{ *from social mixer to kitchen mixer* }

Take your marriage endeavor into forever
With over 800 stores nationwide, a great selection of cherished brands, and the most comprehensive wedding website and registry manager, it's easy to fall in love with Macy's Wedding & Gift Registry.

★macy's
wedding & gift registry
1.800.568.8865

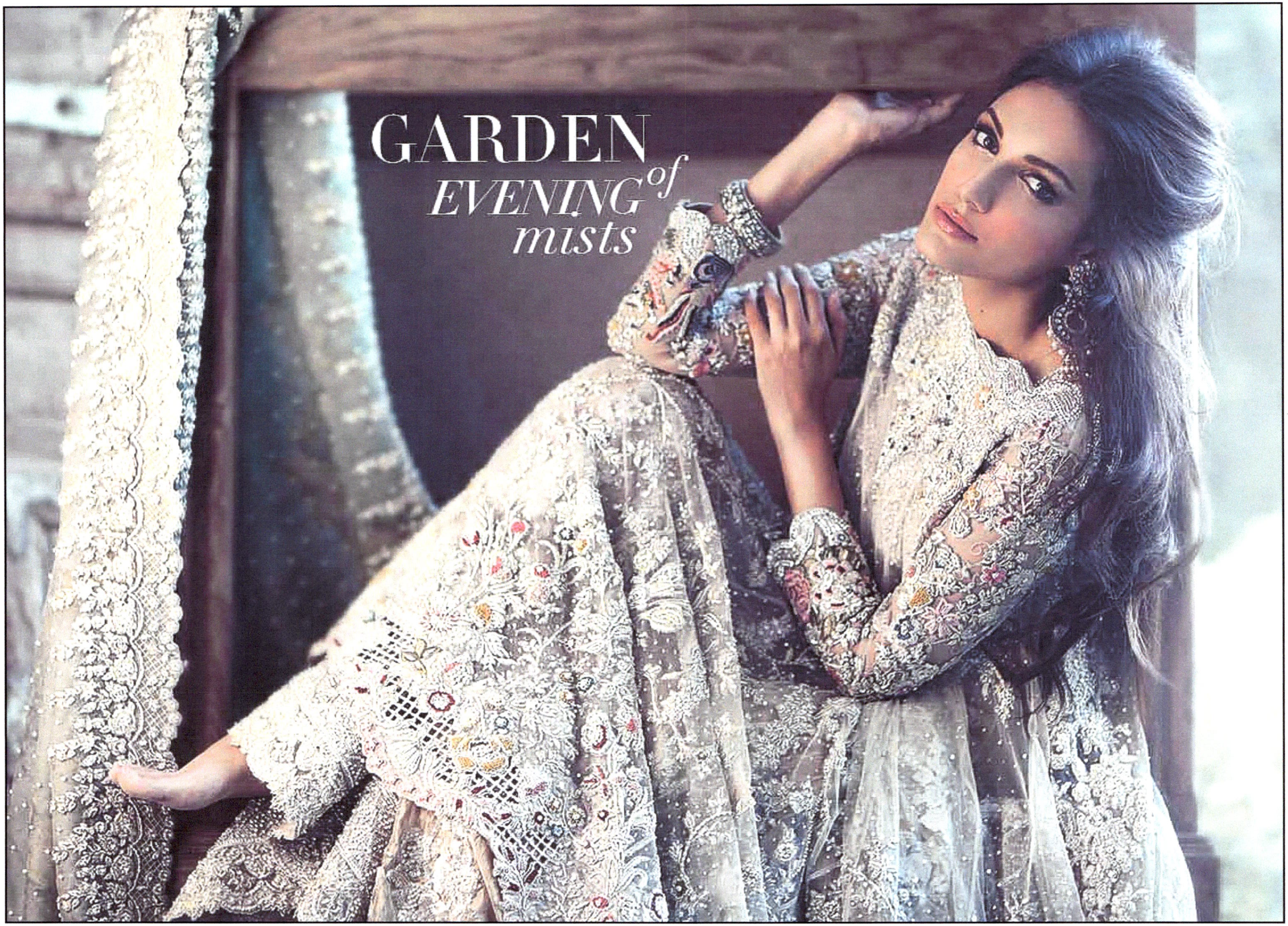
GARDEN of EVENING mists

ROMANCE IN YOUR PATH IDEAS

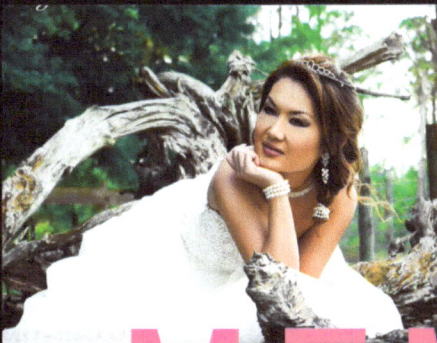

Who is Tenacious Glam?

Tenacious Glam specializes in Luxury Bridal Services. Our team is comprised with over 15 years combined experience in the industry. As a team we are able to accommodate any size wedding and provide punctual and professional services.

How did Tenacious Glam become a vision?

Our journey began in July of 2000 when Tina and Patricia Gay opened Tenacious Tan + Spa a full service salon in Cocoa, Florida. After many years of providing salon services and the growing need in the bridal industry for on location makeup and hair services Tenacious Glam was born in 2010. Tina takes great pride in her company and personally trains and certifies each hair and makeup artist to create a unified team.

Where do you provide services?

Tenacious Glam provides on location hair and makeup services 365 days of the year to the bride and her party anywhere in the United States. We have our home salon in Cocoa, Florida and we opened our second location which is run by our Vice President Brittany Gay in New York in 2014.

What brand of makeup do you use?

Tenacious Glam's President Tina Gay and Vice President Brittany Gay developed their own brand of makeup TG Cosmetics. After many years of using any and all brands of makeup they decided to launch their own to get the coverage they wanted with a foundation and highly pigmented colors that accentuate ones features. It truly will change your life.

Photo by: Captured Souls Photography

Florida

GOWN BY THE KINGS DAUGHTER BRIDAL BOUTIQUE
GINO CERRUTI COLLECTION
PHOTOGRAPHY BY AARON WILLIAMSON
HAIR & MAKEUP BY TENACIOUS GLAM
MODEL SHIANNE DELACRUZ

Miss Cuppy Cakes
by Glenda
321.394.8258

misscuppycakesfl@gmail.com
www.facebook.com/misscuppycakesfl

Enjoy a CUPCAKE

Dreamer
Collection

Kiyonna
Amour Lace Wedding Gown
Style No.: 14130905
www.kiyonna.com

MoriLee
Julietta Collection
Style No: 3176
www.morilee.com

Gino Cerruti
Style No: 31A
www.ginocerruti.com

Roz la Kelin Bridal
Glamour Plus Collection
Style No: Cressida
Style Code: 5935T
www.rozlakelin.com

Allure Bridal
Allure Women Collection
Style No: W374
www.allurebridals.com

Alfred Angelo
Style No: 964
www.alfredangelo.com

Model Usman Tiger

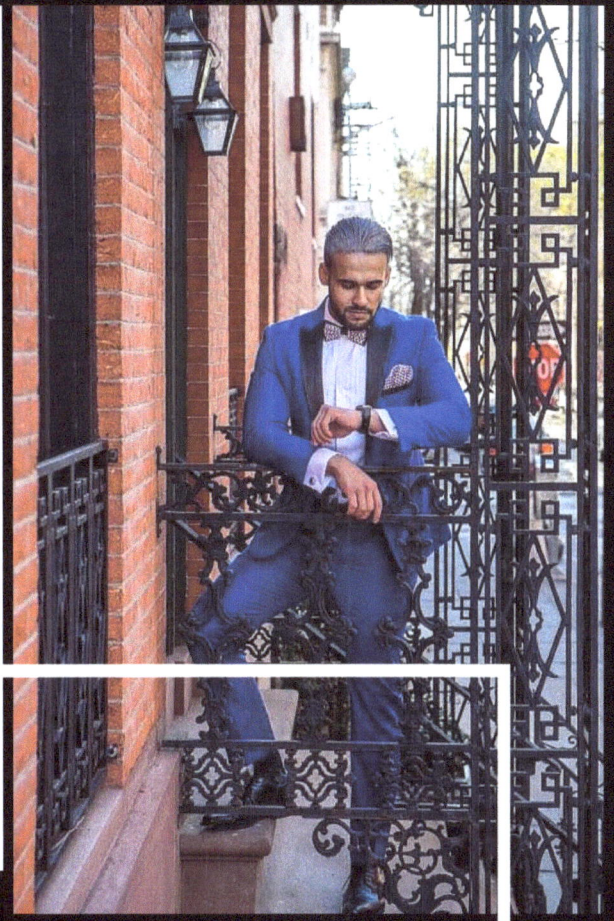

SPICE
THINGS UP with colour

Photography by Luba Fayngersh

lubaphoto.com

Georgia

GOWN BY DAVIDS BRIDAL
VERA WANG
PHOTOGRAPHER SHAWN ROCHELLE PHOTOGRAPHY LLC
MODEL UNIQUA CAMPBELL

THE
BILTMORE

formally yours

BRIDALS & FORMALS

SINCE 1982

---

formallyyoursga.com
info@formallyyoursga.com
770.923.5800

LIGHT *Painting*

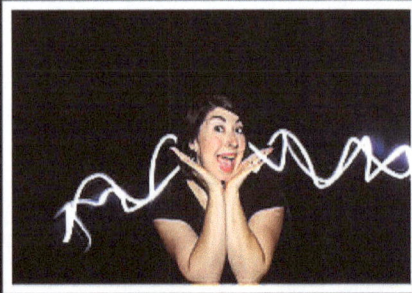

shutter booth sb .com

Social

4 hours of service
10ft x 10ft blackout canopy
Assortment of painting tools
2 ShutterBooth hosts
Unlimited Photo Sessions
Custom logo overlay
Online photo gallery
iPad sharing station (1 iPad)

$1599

Print

4 hours of service
10ft x 10ft blackout canopy
Assortment of painting tools
2 ShutterBooth hosts
Unlimited Photo Sessions
Custom logo overlay
Online photo gallery
On-Site Printing
Unlimited Re-Prints

$1799

Print + Social

4 hours of service
10ft x 10ft blackout canopy
Assortment of painting tools
3 ShutterBooth hosts
Unlimited Photo Sessions
Custom logo overlay
Online photo gallery
HD wall projection of photos
iPad sharing station (3 iPads)
On-Site Printing
Unlimited Re-Prints

$1999

Illinois

GOWN BY DEARBORN TUXEDOS

MAKEUP BY AIESHA RUSS

PHOTOGRAPHY BY SLY FOX PHOTOGRAPHY

MODEL LAURYN CLARK

Limousine

773.744.9319

Vehicle	Capacity	Consecutive Hrs. Minimum	Price Per Hr.	Color
Lincoln Twon Car	4	3	$60	Black
Suv Gmc	6	3	$75	Black
Mercedez S550	4	3	$95	Black
Lincoln Stretch Town Car	10	3	$95	B/W
Suv Stretch	14	3	$150	B/W
Hummer Stretch	20	3	$200	White
Suv Stretch	24	3	$220	White
Party Bus	24	3	$200	Black
Party Bus	28	3	$225	Black
Party Bus	35	3	$250	Silver

* Pick up and drop off are available (Call for details)

* Rates are exclusive of tax and gratuity, vehicles cannot be loaded beyond seating capacity, other restrictions may apply.

MD
Millenium Decorations & Catering

La Salle LIMOUSINE

Michigan

GOWN BY DEARBORN TUXEDOS

MAKEUP BY AIESHA RUSS

PHOTOGRAPHY BY BN PHOTOGRAPHY

MODEL BENITA CARTER

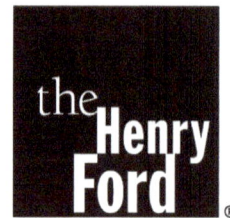

Yasmeena's
Florals

6448 Greenfield Rd, Dearborn MI
(313) 581-1112

DEARBORN TUX

21745 W Warren Ave, Dearborn Heights, MI 48127
Phone:(313) 562-1010

Nevada

GOWN BY THE KINGS DAUGHTER BRIDAL BOUTIQUE
GINO CERRUTI COLLECTION
PHOTOGRAPHY BY AARON WILLIAMSON
HAIR & MAKEUP BY TENACIOUS GLAM
MODEL COURTNEE MEIER

Vegas girls NightOut

vegasgirlsnightout.com

Wellington Place

For couples who are considering hosting their Wedding Ceremony and Reception, or Reception only, we offer a variety of packages according to your needs and desires. Our Venue, which is 14,000 sq ft., offer to Banquet Rooms (on two levels): The La Terrazza Room, which accommodates up to 70 people or our Valencia and Tuscany Rooms, which seat 75 to 250 people. At Wellington Place, we aim to please you, our client. wellingtonplacevegaswedding-300x149We offer Elegant Reception Rooms a beautiful wedding chapel, delicious cakes, appetizers, delicious meals, an awesome DJ/MC, a great staff and much more.

www.vegasweddingreception.com

www.tayloredphotomemories.com

Home of The World's First Elvis Packages!

Viva Las Vegas $199
- Use of Chapel
- Elvis will escort the bride down the aisle and give her away
- Elvis will sing 2 songs
- Rose Presentation
- Rose Boutonniere
- Professional Photography (prints sold separately)

Loving You $329
- Use of Chapel
- Elvis will escort the bride down the aisle and give her away
- Elvis will sing 3 songs
- 3 Rose Nosegay and Rose Boutonniere
- Professional Photography: (6) 4x6's • (1) 8x10
- Certificate Holder

Can't Help Falling in Love $429
- Use of Chapel
- Elvis will escort the bride down the aisle and give her away
- Elvis will sing 3 songs
- 6 Rose Bouquet Rose Boutonniere
- Professional Photography: (6) 4x6's • (2) 5x7's • (1) 8x10
- DVD of Ceremony
- Certificate Holder

Concert with The King $699
- Use of Chapel
- Choice of Elvis Theme: Gold Lamé, Black Leather Jumpsuit or Aloha
- Elvis will escort the bride down the aisle and give her away
- Elvis will sing 5 songs
- Specialty Cascade Bouquet and Boutonniere
- Professional Photography: (12) 4x6's • (6) 5x7's • (3) 8x10's
- DVD of Ceremony
- Certificate Holder

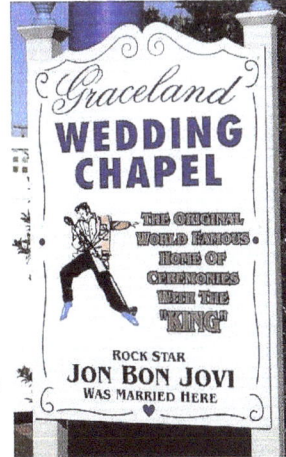

Graceland
WEDDING CHAPEL
THE ORIGINAL WORLD FAMOUS HOME OF CEREMONIES WITH THE "KING"

ROCK STAR JON BON JOVI WAS MARRIED HERE

The Famous Dueling Elvis Package $799
- Use of Chapel
- 2 Different Elvis Impersonators
- Performing 2 Different Stages of Elvis' Career: Gold Lamé Young Elvis and The Flashy Sequined 70's Las Vegas Jumpsuit Elvis!
- 12 Rose Cascade or Hand Tied Bouquet
- Rose Boutonniere
- Professional Photography: (9) 4x6's • (4) 5x7's • (2) 8x10's
- DVD of Ceremony
- Certificate Holder

A STORYBOOK WEDDING CHAPEL

Our Elegant Traditional Packages

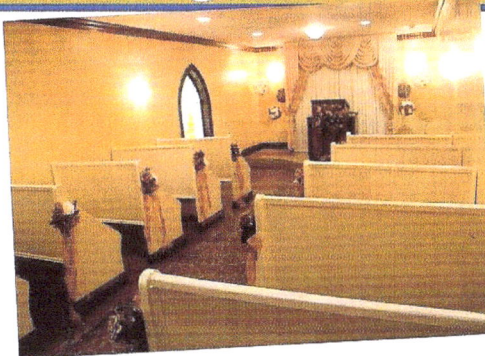

$199.00
- Use of Chapel
- Traditional Wedding Music
- 3 Rose Nosegay and Rose Boutonniere
- Professional Photography: (6) 4x6's • (1) 8x10
- Certificate Holder

$299.00
- Use of Chapel • Traditional Wedding Music
- 6 Rose Bouquet • Rose Boutonniere
- Professional Photography: (6) 4x6's • (2) 5x7's • (1) 8x10
- DVD of Ceremony
- Certificate Holder

$499.00
- Use of Chapel • Traditional Wedding Music
- Specialty Cascade Bouquet and Rose Boutonniere
- Bride's Maid Nosegay Bouquet
- Best Man's Boutonniere
- Professional Photography: (12) 4x6's • (6) 5x7's • (3) 8x10's
- DVD of Ceremony • Certificate Holder

Wedding Ceremonies performed in German, French, Spanish, Italian and Japanese!

$399.00
- Use of Chapel • Traditional Wedding Music
- 12 Rose Cascade or Hand Tied Bouquet
- Rose Boutonniere
- Professional Photography: (9) 4x6's • (4) 5x7's • (2) 8x10's
- DVD of Ceremony
- Certificate Holder

ADDITIONAL CONSIDERATIONS
Minister's Fee: $60 • Photographer's Tip: $20 • Sales Tax
Marriage License: $77 (paid at Marriage Bureau)

**Deposits are Nonrefundable
Prices are Subject to Change
No Substitutions Please**

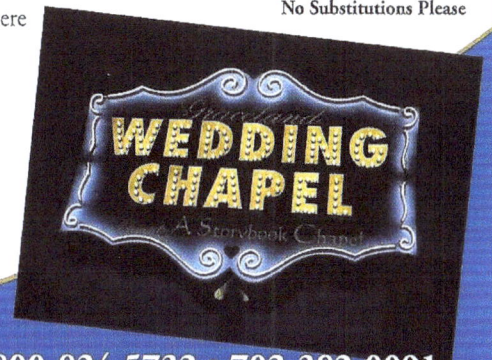

WEDDING CHAPEL
A Storybook Chapel

800-824-5732 • 702-382-0091
619 Las Vegas Blvd. South • Las Vegas, Nevada 89101
www.elvisweddings.com • www.gracelandchapel.com

New York

GINO CERRUTI COLLECTION
PHOTOGRAPHY BY CAPTURED SOULS PHOTOGRAPHY
HAIR & MAKEUP BY TENACIOUS GLAM
MODEL JINI LEE KLUNGLER

Brilliance

It makes sense that the
more radiant the light,
the more vivid the memory.

Wedding Planner: Colin Cowie Celebrations
Photographer: Brian Dorsey Studios
Wedding Venue: New York Public Library
Floral Design and Décor: Colin Cowie Celebrations
Catering: Abigail Kirsh
Entertainment: Empire Entertainment
Lighting: Lighting: L&M Sound & Light
Ice Sculpture: Okamoto Studio

BRIAN DORSEY
STUDIOS

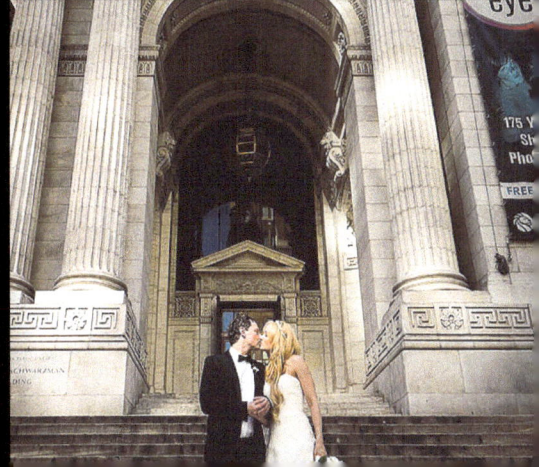

Ohio

GOWN BY THE KINGS DAUGHTER BRIDAL BOUTIQUE
GINO CERRUTI COLLECTION
PHOTOGRAPHY BY JOEY G. NEAS PHOTOGRAPHY

HAIR & MAKEUP BY TENACIOUS GLAM
MODEL JASMINE SPARROW

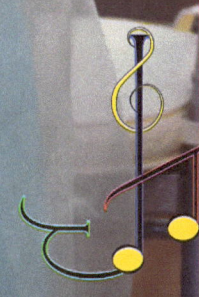

Holiday Inn®
513.657.3835

Maxim
PHOTO STUDIO

bensphotos.com   www.bensphotos.com   McMillen PHOTOGRAPHY   www.bensphotos

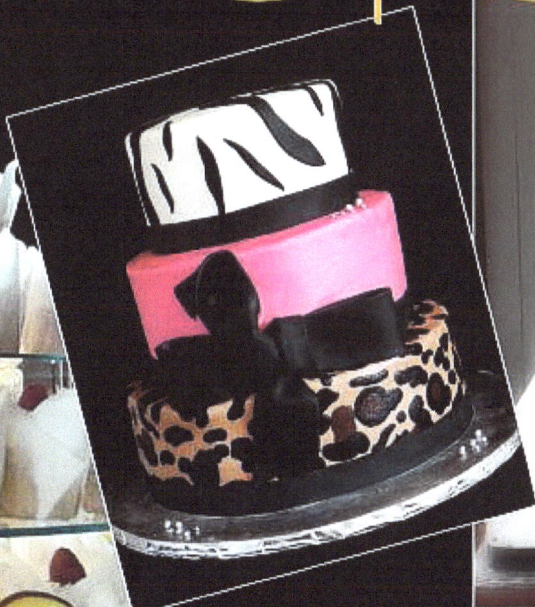

LOVE NEST
DREAM SUITES

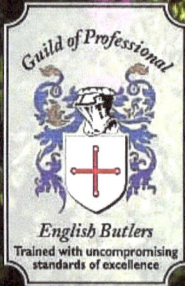

Guild of Professional
English Butlers
Trained with uncompromising
standards of excellence

SUITES
SO ROMANTIC THAT WE CALL THEM
LOVE NESTS

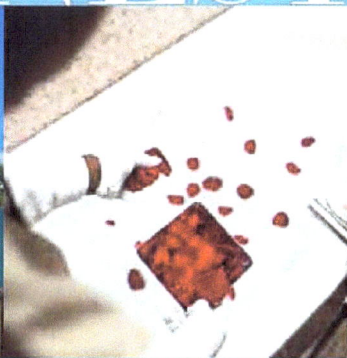

Sandals® Resorts has designed exclusive honeymoon suites and villas that are so exotic, so opulent and so decadently romantic they could only be named "Love Nest Dream Suites." Nowhere else on Earth will you find more original and more luxurious sanctuaries designed for newlyweds to hide away. Sandals has thoughtfully included every sensuous detail from intimate garden grottos and private plunge pools to fully stocked bars and spacious bedrooms with plush beds, oversized spa tubs and walk-in showers built for two. All Love Nest Dream Suites include concierge service, and in top-tier accommodations, 24-hour room service and professionally trained butlers to cater to your every whim. It's the perfect pairing of world-class luxury and island-style romance. In fact, with suites this spectacular and so much to do, many newlyweds never want to leave at all.

ENTER TO WIN◊
a Sandals
Honeymoon!
Monthly drawing at
www.sandals.com/
dreamhoneymoon

Call your Preferred Travel Agent or 1-800-SANDALS or visit sandals.com

*Complimentary with stays of 6 paid nights or more, includes all room categories. All weddings subject to mandatory minister and government documentation fees, which vary by island. All weddings that do not meet the minimum night stay requirement will be subject to a $750 processing and administrative fee, which is inclusive of government and documentation fees. All fees are subject to change at any time. ◊Details, rules and restrictions for monthly honeymoon drawings can be found online at www.sandals.com/dreamhoneymoon. Sandals® is a registered trademark. Unique Vacations, Inc. is the affiliate of the worldwide representative of Sandals Resorts.

Sandals
LOVE IS ALL YOU NEED

Michigan Photoshoot

Model: Alondra Ramos-Herrera

Photographer: BN Photography

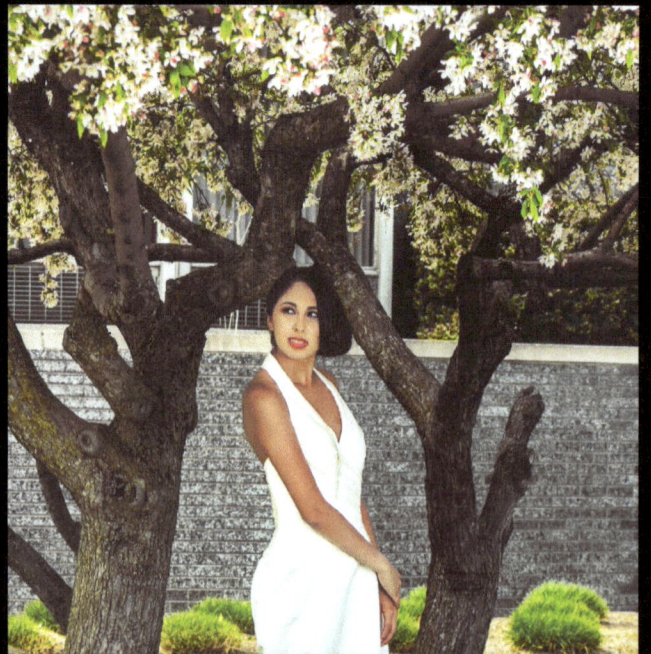

Gino Cerruti
LONDON